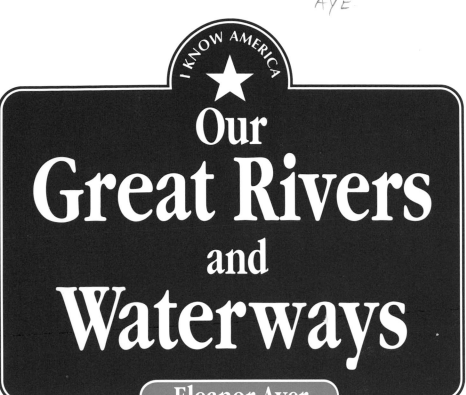

I KNOW AMERICA

Our
Great Rivers
and
Waterways

Eleanor Ayer

THE MILLBROOK PRESS

Brookfield, Connecticut

Published by The Millbrook Press
2 Old New Milford Road
Brookfield, CT 06804
© 1994 Blackbirch Graphics, Inc.

5 4 3 2 1

Created and produced in association with Blackbirch Graphics.
Series Editor: Tanya Lee Stone

Library of Congress Cataloging-in-Publication Data
Ayer, Eleanor H.
    Our great rivers and waterways / by Eleanor Ayer.
        p.   cm. — (I know America)
    Includes bibliographical references and index.
    Summary: Presents our country's great rivers, lakes, and waterways and
describes how people explored, settled, and developed the U.S. interior along
our river system.
    ISBN 1-56294-441-X (lib. bdg.)
    1. Waterways—United States—Juvenile literature. 2. Rivers—United
States—Juvenile literature. 3. United States—Geography—Juvenile literature.
I. Title. II. Series.
E161.3.A94 1994
917.3'09693—dc20
                                                          93-38355
                                                          CIP
                                                          AC

Acknowledgments and Photo Credits
Cover: ©Fred Mayer/Magnum Photos, Inc.; p. 5: ©Dennis Stock/Magnum
Photos, Inc.; p. 6: Photo courtesy of the Washington, D. C. Convention &
Visitors Association; p. 10: ©1986 Will and Deni McIntyre/Photo
Researchers, Inc.; p. 11: ©1984 Hank Morgan/Photo Researchers, Inc.; pp.
12, 17, 18, 20: Library of Congress; p. 14: Leo de Wys, Inc; p. 19: Alabama
Bureau of Tourism and Travel; p. 21: ©Blackbirch Press; p. 22: ©Larry
Mayer/Gamma Liaison Network; pp. 23, 34: National Park Service; p. 24:
Jeff Gnass Photography, Inc.; p. 35: American Rivers Association; p. 27: ©Ed
Lallo/Liaison International; p. 29: North Wind Picture Archives; p. 30:
©Michael Nichols/Magnum Photos; p. 36: ©1986 David Halpern/Photo
Researchers, Inc.; p. 39: Richard Frear/National Park Service; p. 40: New
York State Commerce Department; p. 42: St. Lawrence Seaway
Development Corporation; p. 43: Utah Travel Council.

CONTENTS

Introduction **4**

The Basis of Our River Systems 5

CHAPTER 1 **Exploring Our Eastern Water Routes** **7**

Potomac River 9

Cumberland River 9

Ohio River 10

Tennessee River 11

Eastern Canals 13

Intracoastal Waterway System 13

CHAPTER 2 **The Mighty Mississippi River System** **15**

Discovering the Mississippi 15

"Steamboat A-Comin" 17

Life on the Mississippi 19

The Mississippi River System Today 23

CHAPTER 3 **Following the Mississippi-Missouri's**
Western Tributaries **25**

Platte River 25

Arkansas River 26

Red River 28

Yellowstone River 28

CHAPTER 4 **Discovering Our Western Rivers** **31**

Colorado River 31

Columbia and Snake Rivers 33

Yukon River 35

Rio Grande 35

CHAPTER 5 **America's Lakes** **37**

The Great Lakes 38

Land of 10,000 Lakes 41

The Great Salt Lake 43

America's Longest Rivers **44**

America's Largest Lakes **45**

Chronology **46**

For Further Reading **47**

Index **48**

INTRODUCTION

"About midnight Tom arrived with a boiled ham and a few trifles.... It was starlight, and very still. The mighty river lay like an ocean at rest...."

This "ocean at rest" was the river of Tom Sawyer's and Huckleberry Finn's boyhoods—the Mississippi—which carries water from a third of America's streams and rivers into the Gulf of Mexico. In the mid-nineteenth century, when Tom and Huck were growing up, the Mississippi was an important travel route.

Two hundred years earlier, America's great rivers belonged to the wilderness and to Native Americans, who called the Mississippi "The Father of Waters." In those days there were no factories, no power plants, and no large settlements along the riverbanks.

This solitude was broken when white people discovered what wonderful routes rivers made for exploring North America. From the South and West came Spanish explorers, looking for gold and new lands. From the North and East came the French and English, lured by the wealth of furs to be trapped along the rivers' banks. They opened the way for settlement of the United States by the whites.

As towns and villages grew, people began using the rivers for business. Up and down the waters they traveled, trading goods and moving people into unsettled lands. They also floated their cargo on the nation's lakes, which made good transportation routes before there were railroads or highways.

But traveling long distances often required moving goods overland between bodies of water. To tackle this difficult chore, people built canals— waterways to connect the natural bodies of water.

The Basis of Our River Systems

All rivers in the United States eventually end up in either the Atlantic Ocean (directly, or by way of the Gulf of Mexico) or the Pacific Ocean. Which ocean a river empties into is decided by an imaginary line that runs roughly along the crest of the Rocky Mountains. This line is called the Continental Divide, and although it is imaginary, you can stand "atop" it at many points in the western United States. Rivers east of the Divide flow into the Atlantic Ocean and rivers west of the Divide flow into the Pacific Ocean.

Running down the heart of the United States from the northern part of the country south to the Gulf of Mexico is the Mississippi River system. This is the longest and most important river system in the United States. It includes the Mississippi River and its many tributaries (bodies of water that flow into it). To the east and west of the Mississippi River system are many other rivers, as well as streams, canals, and other waterways. This book will describe some of the most important bodies of water in the country.

The Colorado River is one of America's most beautiful waterways. The U.S. government has passed laws to preserve the natural beauty of our rivers.

5

EXPLORING OUR EASTERN WATER ROUTES

In 1609, an adventurous twelve-year-old boy named Henry Spelman ran away from his home in England. After arriving at Plymouth, in what is today the state of Massachusetts, Henry sneaked aboard the *Unity*, a ship headed for the Virginia colony of Jamestown. At Jamestown, Captain John Smith, who had helped to found the colony, became his friend. Smith arranged for Henry to live in Indian country.

While there, Henry became fascinated with the rivers and the areas they led to. He was the first white person to explore the headwaters (places where rivers begin) of the James River, the Potomac River, and the other rivers that enter Chesapeake Bay. Like his historian father, he kept detailed records. But Henry's adventurous spirit would soon land him in trouble.

Opposite:
A crew team rows on the Potomac River near Georgetown University in Washington, D.C.

7

On a trip down the Potomac in 1622, he and his crew were attacked by members of the Anacostan tribe. During the battle, Henry was killed.

Exploration of the eastern rivers continued for many years after Henry Spelman's death. The colonists were very interested in finding out what lay farther west. Boats traveling up the Hudson River brought settlers to the mouth of the Mohawk River, which led to the Ohio Valley by way of Lake Ontario. The Susquehanna and Monongahela rivers allowed people from Pennsylvania and Maryland to cross the Allegheny Mountains. And from the valley of Virginia settlers picked up the Tennessee and Cumberland rivers on their way west.

Some Important Rivers of the East

Area of Detail

Hudson River
Penobscot River
ME
VT
NH
Connecticut River
NY
MA
CT
RI
Allegheny River
Susquehanna River
Delaware River
Monongahela River
PA
NJ
OH
MD
Schuylkill River
DE
IL
IN
Ohio River
Potomac River
VA
KY
WV
James River
Chesapeake Bay
Cumberland River
Roanoke River
NC
TN
Tennessee River
Savannah River
SC
Tombigbee River
AL
Alabama River
Chattahoochee River
GA
MS
Atlantic Ocean
St. John River
FL
Gulf of Mexico
Kissimmee River
Lake Okeechobee

Potomac River

The river that so fascinated Henry Spelman is noted for its beauty and its significance in the history of the United States. The Potomac flows about 285 miles from its source in the Appalachian Mountains to empty into Chesapeake Bay.

Mount Vernon, the home of the country's first president, George Washington, is located on the Potomac, south of Washington, D.C., in the state of Virginia. Washington was especially interested in the Potomac as a commercial river route. Today, the Potomac remains a central element in our nation's capital. In addition to providing scenic beauty and recreation for the Washington-Delaware-Maryland region, the Potomac is also navigable by large vessels transporting materials throughout the area.

Cumberland River

The Cumberland River played an important role during the Civil War. During this conflict, the South tried to protect the river by building Fort Donelson at the point where the Cumberland River re-enters Kentucky. The Southern army also built Fort Henry on the Tennessee River, which is nearby. In February of 1862, the North won its first major battle of the war there, when General Ulysses S. Grant captured both forts. This gave Union forces a water route into the South.

The winding 687-mile Cumberland rises in the Cumberland Mountains of eastern Kentucky, flows through Tennessee, and then re-enters Kentucky at

The largest city located along the Cumberland River is Nashville, Tennessee, with a population of more than 510,000.

Smithfield to empty into the Ohio River. It cuts through the famous Cumberland Gap, which was used as a route to the West by the pioneers.

Today, the river is a source of hydroelectric power (electricity produced by waterpower) and controls floods with its many dams. Barges traveling down the Cumberland carry—among other items—steel, food, chemicals, and petroleum products.

Ohio River

The mighty Ohio River begins right in the heart of Pittsburgh, Pennsylvania. It is formed at the meeting point of two other big eastern rivers, the Allegheny and the Monongahela. From here, the Ohio travels 981 miles south and west along the West Virginia, Ohio, Kentucky, Indiana, and Illinois borders until it empties into the Mississippi at Cairo, Illinois. Because it empties into the Mississippi, the Ohio is considered a tributary of the Mississippi.

The Iroquois Indians used this waterway long before white explorers did. In fact, *Ohio* is an Iroquois word that means "fine" or "great" river. In time, the Ohio River became a major water route for settlers heading into the wilderness of southern Ohio, West Virginia, Kentucky, Indiana, Illinois, and Tennessee. As farming and business grew, the river became important for shipping.

Today, barges carry oil, gas, gravel, steel, and chemicals along the river. Because icy conditions do not prevent boat travel during the winter, as is the case with some rivers, the Ohio is one of the country's most important year-round transportation routes.

Tennessee River

The Tennessee flows through the states of Tennessee, Alabama, and Kentucky. Once a major eastern river and a tributary of the Ohio, it is now more of a chain of lakes and dams than a free-flowing river. The change began in 1933, when the government, under President Franklin D. Roosevelt, set up the Tennessee Valley Authority (TVA). The purposes of the TVA were to control flooding, improve navigation on the river, and produce electric power.

When a dam is built on a river, a lake or reservoir is formed behind it. The dams along the Tennessee River made many new lakes. A series of locks connects these lakes, allowing the water level to be raised or lowered so that boats can travel between them.

The Norris Dam is one of the nearly thirty dams that make up the TVA.

THE ERIE CANAL

Since 1609, when Henry Hudson first sailed up its waters in the *Half Moon,* the Hudson River has been a major waterway in eastern New York. It is the route of much travel between the capital at Albany and the river's mouth in New York City. Explorers and traders had long seen the need for a canal to connect the Hudson River with Lake Erie, one of the Great Lakes, near today's city of Buffalo, New York. Such a canal would open the West to growth and settlement.

In 1817, digging began on the Erie Canal. Eight years later, in 1825, the completed canal, running 364 miles between Albany and Buffalo, connected the Great Lakes with the Atlantic Ocean. For most of its length, the canal is 150 feet wide and runs about 13 feet deep.

In the early years, mules walking on towpaths along the banks pulled the barges. A popular song of the day began, *"I had a mule and her name was Sal, sixteen years on the Erie Canal...."* Not until the early 1900s did canal boats have their own gasoline or steam-powered engines.

The Erie Canal remained a major shipping route into the twentieth century. Products from factories and mills in the Great Lakes region were loaded on barges and taken across the Erie Canal to Albany, then down the Hudson River to New York. Over the years, other rivers and canals were connected to the Erie. The result was the New York State Barge Canal System, one of the longest waterways in America. Although freight traffic has declined from the Erie Canal's busiest days, more than 100,000 vessels still travel its waters each year.

Eastern Canals

The problem of traveling between America's lakes and rivers troubled boatmen for years. In 1690, William Penn, founder of Philadelphia, had the idea for building a waterway to connect the Delaware River and its tributary, the Schuylkill, with the Susquehanna River near Chesapeake Bay. This was the first of more than 4,000 miles of canals that would one day link rivers and lakes in the northeastern United States.

Canals made it possible to ship goods entirely by boat, without having to change to other kinds of transportation. "Packets," as the canal boats were called, boasted top speeds of four miles an hour. Canals connected the villages along their routes and opened up new frontiers for settlement.

Intracoastal Waterway System

A water route that is sheltered from the coast and connected by various bodies of water, such as rivers, bays, and canals, is called an intracoastal waterway. An intracoastal waterway provides storm-free passage for pleasure boats and cargo-carrying vessels.

The 3,000 miles of the Atlantic Intracoastal Waterway and the Gulf Intracoastal Waterway make up the Intracoastal Waterway System of America.

The 1,900-mile Atlantic Intracoastal Waterway stretches from Boston, Massachusetts, to Key West, Florida. The 1,100-mile Gulf Intracoastal Waterway extends from Apalachee Bay on Florida's west coast to Brownsville, Texas.

CHAPTER 2

THE MIGHTY MISSISSIPPI RIVER SYSTEM

Of all the rivers in the world, only the Nile in Africa and the Amazon in South America are longer than the Mississippi River system. This system includes the Mississippi River, the Missouri River (its chief tributary), and hundreds of other tributaries. Cutting a path through the center of the United States, the system carries water from thirty-one states and two Canadian provinces southward into the Gulf of Mexico.

Discovering the Mississippi

In the days before Europeans came to the New World, Native Americans lived peacefully along the banks of the Mississippi River. Here they farmed the land and traveled the river from one village to the next. They worshipped the spirit and power of the Great River.

Opposite:
The Mississippi River is one of the most traveled rivers in the world.

15

As outsiders ventured into North America, they also recognized the power and promise of the Mississippi. Spanish explorer Hernando de Soto was the first European to sight the southern Mississippi in 1541, while on a gold-seeking expedition. He died a year later, along its banks, never having found gold.

More than a century later, in 1673, French explorers Louis Jolliet and Father Jacques Marquette discovered the river's northern stretch. Marquette was a priest, who had come to convert the Native Americans to the religion of the white people. Jolliet hoped to build a great empire in the New World.

Jolliet never built his empire. Another man, René-Robert Cavelier, sieur de La Salle, was chosen

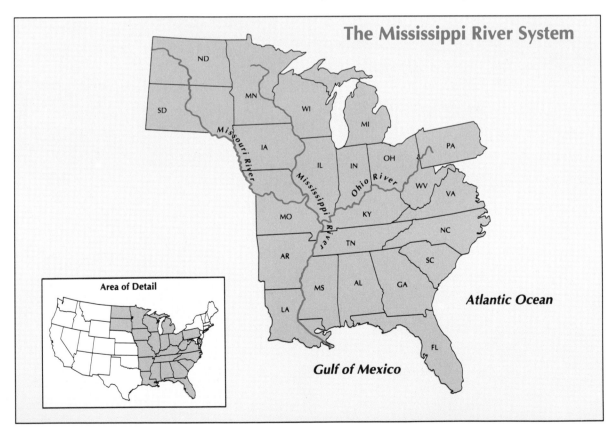

The Mississippi River System

by the French government to explore the Mississippi Valley. La Salle headed south, searching for the Mississippi's mouth. When he found it, in 1682, he claimed the Mississippi River basin for France.

La Salle set up the first of many businesses along the river, a series of trading stations for trappers. Along the Missouri River and its tributaries, these mountain men journeyed west to trap the animals whose pelts were prized by Easterners for making hats and clothing. When the mountain men returned, they stopped to trade their furs for cash or supplies.

Hernando de Soto.

Even though La Salle had claimed the area for France, the Spanish kept control of the lower Mississippi until 1800. In that year, Spain gave up the territory of Louisiana to the French, leaving France to rule the river. The United States immediately sent a messenger to Paris, offering to buy the land drained by the Mississippi. The French were willing to sell, and by the end of December 1803, the United States had made the Louisiana Purchase, one of the greatest real estate deals in history. Land that would one day form thirteen U.S. states was purchased for just $15 million.

"Steamboat A-Comin"

In 1811, a series of earthquakes shook the land near where the Ohio River joins the Mississippi. These earthquakes changed the river's route. New islands were born, while others disappeared. Riverbanks were moved, and bluffs were destroyed, as more than a million square miles of land churned and shifted.

Caught in the river's violent lurching was the *New Orleans,* the first steamboat to travel on the Mississippi-Missouri system. Its designer, Nicholas Roosevelt, had taken his idea for a steamboat from eastern inventor Robert Fulton. Just four years earlier, in 1807, Fulton had tested his invention, the *Clermont,* along the Hudson River in New York. By 1820, more than seventy-five steamboats were chugging up and down the Mississippi.

These first steamers were little more than flatboats with an engine and a paddle wheel on the side. Boilers in the bottom heated water to produce steam, which was put under pressure to power the engine. Gradually these ugly ducklings evolved into luxury liners. They had beautiful brass fixtures, elegant bedrooms and ballrooms, and the power to reach speeds not previously known on the river.

Encouraged by their success on the Mississippi, boatmen decided to head west, and in 1831 regular steamboat service began on the Missouri River. But the shallow waters and sandbars of the Missouri made steamboat travel more difficult than on the Mississippi. What was needed to navigate these waters was a boat with the paddle wheel in the back—a stern-wheeler. They were smaller, slower, and less luxurious than the sidewheelers. But they sat higher in the water and were not as likely to get stuck in the Missouri's mud, sandbars, and weeds.

Steamboats turned the Mississippi and Missouri rivers into America's most traveled water routes.

Southern plantation owners relied on them to move the huge amounts of cotton they raised. In the years before the Civil War, the steamboat was the queen of the Mississippi, and cotton was king. Field workers— usually African-American slaves—hauled bales of cotton on wagons to landings along the river. There they waited for steamboats that would carry the loads to their destinations.

Life on the Mississippi

All kinds of colorful characters lived along the Mississippi and in fast-growing river towns like St. Louis, Missouri, Natchez, Mississippi, and Memphis, Tennessee. The rowdy crewmen of the keelboats and flatboats now shared the river with dignified steamboat pilots. Along the shore, workmen at docking stations prepared to help service the boat, unload its cargo, or restock it with wood for the boiler room.

Many children who lived along the banks of the Mississippi (nicknamed Old Man River) in the late

By the mid-1800s, stern-wheelers were the new ugly ducklings of the rivers. This one, the *General Richard Montgomery*, is a replica of a stern-wheeler.

FLATBOATS AND KEELBOATS

Throughout its long history, the Mississippi-Missouri system has been a water highway for carrying people and products. Native Americans and early explorers traveled in simple canoes. As the need for larger boats arose, people modified the design of the canoe, making the bottom flatter, more stable, and able to carry heavier loads. These flatboats carried as much as fifteen tons of freight for a cost of two dollars a day. They were powered by boatmen who paddled with oars or stuck poles into the water to push their craft along.

As boat design improved, keelboats came into use. Some curved upward on the ends, somewhat like a canoe, and had a cabin in the center. Keelboats were powered by a sail when there was wind. This allowed them to move upriver, against the current, nearly as easily as downstream. When there was no wind, however, their crews had to paddle or pole their craft like flatboats. Fully loaded boats often had to be pulled by sturdy boatmen wading in water up to their waists or necks.

These river boatmen were mainly good-natured Frenchmen, a rough and rowdy bunch, who played cards, gambled, and drank whiskey. But they also worked very hard. The job of moving heavily loaded boats through the water took a long time, and it was tiring and highly dangerous.

nineteenth century dreamed of working on a steamboat. For long hours each day they would play on the bluffs above the river, just waiting for a boat to pull into the landing. One of those children, Samuel Clemens, worked as a Mississippi steamboat pilot as an adult, and he wrote about his experiences in the book *Life on the Mississippi*. But it was the characters in two of his other books that would make him famous. Huck Finn and Tom Sawyer are patterned after Clemens's own boyhood friends in Hannibal, Missouri. The name Mark Twain, under which Clemens wrote, also comes from the river. "Mark Twain" was the call that Mississippi River pilots shouted when they measured the river's water depth and found it to be "two fathoms deep."

As the river towns grew, people opened blacksmith shops, post offices, banks, restaurants, taverns, and other businesses. Dance-hall girls entertained riverboat passengers and crewmen. Cigar-smoking, whiskey-drinking gamblers gathered in the saloons or aboard the steamboats every night to try their luck at cards and other games.

But during the Civil War, life along the river changed. One part of the Mississippi was controlled by the North, and the other by the South. Throughout the four-year-long war, the river was used to carry soldiers, ammunition, and other supplies. The Mississippi's beautiful boats were sunk by gunboats or were set afire to prevent them from falling into the hands of the enemy. Others were tied up and

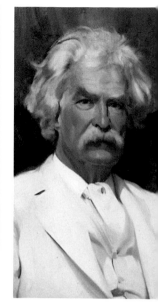

Samuel Clemens lived in the river town of Hannibal, Missouri, as a child.

When heavy rains or melting snow swell rivers and lakes beyond their banks, when dams burst or levees break, waters surge out of their boundaries and flood the countryside. Flood damage is measured in two ways: the cost in human lives and the cost in dollars.

In the summer of 1993, a flood more damaging in terms of dollar damage than any before it hit the United States. Record-breaking snowfall in the northern and Rocky Mountains had the Missouri River and its tributaries running high by late spring. During June and July, heavy rain fell over parts of nine states through which the upper Mississippi and Missouri rivers flow. So great was the force of the Missouri as it rushed east to meet the Mississippi that it cut a new channel 20 miles upstream from where the rivers normally meet. When the Mississippi finally crested in St. Louis, Missouri, it was nearly 48 feet deep—18 feet above flood level and just 4 feet below the 52-foot-high flood wall built to hold back the

Burlington, Iowa, during the 1993 flood.

river from the city. A number of people lost their lives, and damage was estimated in the billions.

eventually rotted. After the war, the river was in bad shape. The levee system built for flood control had been ruined during the four long years of neglect. Steamboat travel along both the Mississippi and Missouri declined.

The Mississippi River System Today

By the 1870s, railroads were running across the East and Midwest, and farmers and businesspeople began using them to ship their products. Passengers discovered that trains were faster than ships, even if they weren't as luxurious a way to travel.

For one type of shipping, however, the river remained very important. Barges—flat-bottomed boats that are sometimes towed by tugboats—came into use for hauling coal, oil, sand, gravel, cotton, and other products along the great Mississippi-Missouri river route. Barges remain in wide use today, and the mighty Mississippi River system is still one of the world's busiest waterways.

The Missouri River is so murky that it has been given the nickname, "Big Muddy."

FOLLOWING THE MISSISSIPPI-MISSOURI'S WESTERN TRIBUTARIES

The major route to the great American West was the Missouri River and its tributaries. Explorers, fur traders, and pioneers headed up the Missouri and from there traveled the rivers that run through today's Great Plains and Rocky Mountain states.

Platte River

The Platte, meaning "flat" in French, is a shallow body of water filled with sandbars. The valley formed a natural transportation route. It was picked up by pioneers just south of Omaha, in the well-named town of Plattsmouth, Nebraska, where it empties into the Missouri. From here the pioneers headed west along the Platte's 310 miles toward today's city of North

Opposite:
The Yellowstone River flows through Yellowstone National Park in Wyoming.

25

Platte, where the river divides into the North Platte and South Platte rivers. Those following the northern route went west into Wyoming along the 600 miles of the North Platte. The settlers on the southern route followed the 450-mile South Platte into Colorado. In spite of its shallowness and the sandbars, the Platte was perhaps the most important river in the opening of the West.

Arkansas River

The Arkansas is another river that brought many explorers and settlers through the rugged west. It flows about 1,450 miles from the Colorado Rockies east through Kansas, Oklahoma, and Arkansas to empty into the Mississippi. Where the Arkansas

River tumbles out of the Colorado mountains, it cuts a spectacular canyon, the Royal Gorge, which is sometimes called the Grand Canyon of the Arkansas. The Denver & Rio Grande Railroad winds through the bottom of this canyon. Spanning the river, 1,053 feet above, is the famous Royal Gorge Bridge, the world's

The Arkansas River flows through Oklahoma on its way to the Mississippi.

highest suspension bridge. This bridge makes it possible for people to walk or drive across the canyon. Explorer Zebulon Pike and his men were searching for the source of the Arkansas in 1806 when they first sighted the mountain that now bears Pike's name.

Red River

The Red River, also called Red River of the South (there is a Red River of the North, which rises in Minnesota and flows into Canada), is about 1,300 miles long. Experts disagree on just where this river begins. Some say it rises near Vernon, Texas, where two creeks come together. Others say it begins in the high plains of eastern New Mexico. Wherever its source, the river runs east, through Texas and then to Louisiana. About 500 miles of it form the border between Texas and Oklahoma.

The Red River helped to open the area to cattlemen and ranchers in the late 1800s. Many of the big trails along which the cattle drives took place, like the famous Chisholm Trail, crossed the Red River. As they drove their herds north to be sold, the cowboys would sit around their campfires at night and sing: *"Remember the Red River Valley, and the cowboy who loved you so true."*

Yellowstone River

The Yellowstone was one of the rivers that eastern fur trappers traveled in their search for beaver pelts. John Colter first explored the Yellowstone River in 1807.

This engraving
showing visitors
at Yellowstone
Lake was done in
1882.

He had been with Lewis and Clark when they
ventured through the wild and unsettled Louisiana
Territory between 1803 and 1806. A year later, he
returned to scout the area for furs—and for Indians.
Colter thus became the first white person to visit what
would one day be Yellowstone National Park, through
which the river flows.

The 671-mile Yellowstone rises in northwestern
Wyoming, close to the Continental Divide, and flows
north into the park. Within the park it creates the
beautiful Yellowstone Lake. The river's colorful
canyon north of the lake is one of the park's most
spectacular scenic features. The river did not get its
name from the canyon, however, but from the yellow
banks at the point where it joins the Missouri River.

DISCOVERING OUR WESTERN RIVERS

The western rivers of America established important transportation routes that led to increased fur trapping and trading activity. These routes also allowed explorers to lead new expeditions into uncharted territories and provided a path for gold miners to follow and seek their fortune.

Colorado River

The forming of the Grand Canyon began more than a million years ago, when the waters of the Colorado River began cutting into the colorful sandstone, shale, and limestone of the Colorado Plateau in northern Arizona. Today the Grand Canyon is the world's most complex system of canyons and gorges, with many

Opposite:
Boating is popular on the Colorado River. The Colorado rises in Grand Lake, high in the Rocky Mountains, and empties into the Gulf of California.

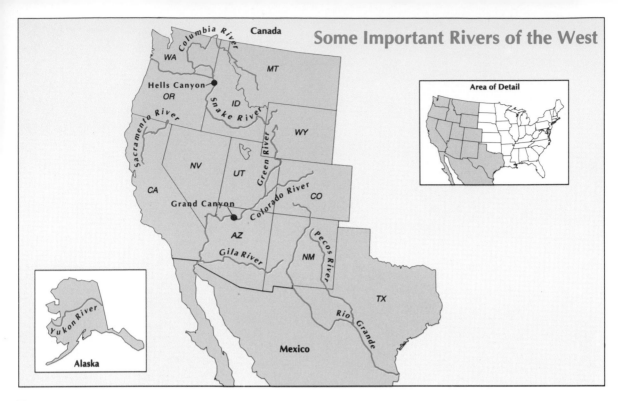

side canyons branching off the main channel. At its widest point the Grand Canyon is about 18 miles across and more than 1 mile deep. Over the years, dirt and rock has been washed away by the river as it cut the canyon—enough to cover the whole United States with a layer more than 1 foot deep.

The Grand Canyon gets its name not only because it is big, but also because the Colorado River, which cuts it, used to be called the Grand River. For much of its route this river travels through some of the most spectacular canyons in the world.

Canyonlands National Park in Utah is known for the beautiful canyons cut by the Colorado and its largest tributary, the Green River. From here, the river heads southwest into spectacular Glen Canyon, also carved by the Colorado. Between 1956 and 1964 the government worked on the construction of Glen Canyon Dam on the river in north central Arizona. The dam created Lake Powell, named for explorer John Wesley Powell, leader of the first expedition (1869) to travel the length of the Colorado by boat and the first to explore the Grand Canyon.

Columbia and Snake Rivers

The Columbia River, along with the Snake River, its largest tributary, was the scene of tremendous fur trapping and trading activity during the early nineteenth century. Both British and American companies fought for control of this huge fur empire.

The Columbia River rises in a small lake in southwestern Canada. It forms the border between Washington and Oregon for much of its 1,210 miles before emptying into the Pacific Ocean. This river dumps almost as much water into the ocean as the Mississippi. Its power has been used to produce electricity, and it has supplied water to farmlands.

The Snake River, one of America's largest and most beautiful river systems, rises in the southeastern section of Yellowstone National Park in Wyoming on the west side of the Continental Divide. Flowing from Wyoming, the river then snakes through Idaho, Oregon, and Washington, where it empties into the Columbia River. On its 1,038-mile journey, the mighty river flows through deep gorges and tumbles down breathtaking waterfalls to create Hells Canyon, the deepest river gorge in North America.

The Grand Coulee Dam.

The flow of many western rivers has been changed by dams. Dams were built to control floods and provide electric power.

Because the West is extremely dry, water is very important to farmers and ranchers as well as to city dwellers. Water rights have long been a source of conflict in the West. If a river flows past your farm, you do not necessarily have the right to use it. The right is decided by government rules that say just how much water can be taken from which points and by whom.

Perhaps because it has more dams than any other river in the world, the Colorado has been at the center of many arguments over water rights. Seven major dams and many smaller ones have changed the river's flow. The most famous of these is Hoover Dam on the Arizona-Nevada border. At first called Boulder Dam, it was built in 1936 to provide electric power. Behind the dam, Lake Mead formed. Other big dams send Colorado River water to cities and farms in California.

The Columbia is another heavily dammed river. The largest of its dams is the Grand Coulee, west of Spokane, Washington, which sends irrigation water and electric power to a wide area.

Irrigation water from damming the Snake River has turned Idaho's desert country into beautiful farmland. Thanks to dams, people living along the Snake have nearly 100 percent of their electric power supplied by the river.

Despite these benefits, dams have caused some serious problems for both people and the environment. Dams have diminished wetlands and interfered with wildlife. The reservoirs created by dams have covered farmlands. Faulty dam construction has resulted in flooding during severe storms, and construction of the dams themselves has required that families move from their homes.

Yukon River

The Yukon River, in Canada and Alaska, also lured men of the fur trade. Trappers for the Hudson's Bay Company worked their way along the Yukon River into Canada's Yukon Territory. Later, the Yukon became a travel route for gold seekers rushing to the Klondike in the Yukon Territory in 1897. In modern times, the Yukon served as an important waterway when oil exploration was taking place on Alaska's North Slope. Even so, the Yukon remains one of the least explored waterways on our continent.

Rising in British Columbia, Canada, the 1,979-mile Yukon is the longest river in Alaska and the third longest river in the United States. On its journey, it passes through many different kinds of terrain—mountains, valleys, rocky gorges, lakes shaped like fingers, sandbars, low islands covered with willow, spruce and birch trees, and marshlands.

Rio Grande

The Rio Grande, meaning "big river" in Spanish, rises in the Colorado mountains, not far from the sources of the Arkansas. The 1,800-mile-long Rio Grande then travels south and east, emptying into the Gulf of Mexico near Brownsville, Texas. The river is most famous where it runs through Texas, for here it forms the border between Mexico and the United States.

The spectacular Rio Grande is the fifth-longest river in North America.

AMERICA'S LAKES

Not all the travel, exploration, and settlement on America's waterways occurred along the rivers. The United States has thousands of lakes, some natural and some built by engineers. Many lakes are really reservoirs that were created to store water, provide electric power, or offer scenic spots for recreation. The Great Lakes, all of them natural, are by far the largest in the country. They touch eight states and the province of Ontario, Canada.

Of the five Great Lakes, Superior is the biggest, followed by Lake Huron, Lake Michigan, Lake Erie, and Lake Ontario. Among the other notable American lakes are the many lakes of Minnesota, often called the "10,000 Lakes," and Utah's Great Salt Lake.

Opposite:
The north shoreline of Lake Superior has a rugged beauty. The entire Great Lakes region is known for its wealth of natural resources— forests, iron ore, copper, and limestone.

37

The Great Lakes

The Great Lakes region is the most important economic area in eastern North America. Control of the lakes has been shared by the United States and Canada, and both countries have helped develop the region. Big businesses like auto companies, factories, and farms are located there. Nearly half the people in the country live in the eight states touched by the Great Lakes. These lakes are all connected to each other. In some places they are linked by rivers, lakes, or canals, and in others they are naturally connected to each other. This allows ships to travel from the Midwest all the way to the Atlantic Ocean in the East, making the Great Lakes region the busiest inland (surrounded by land) water route in the world.

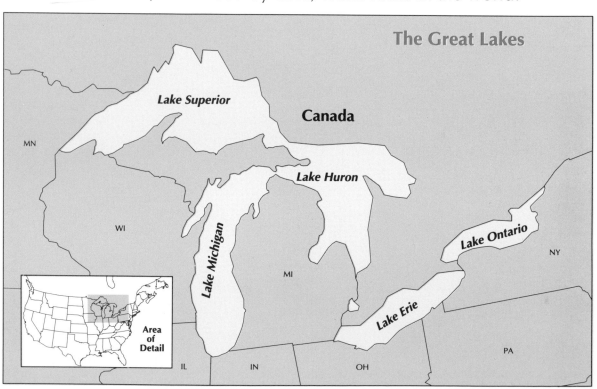

The Great Lakes

Lake Superior, in addition to being the largest of the Great Lakes, is the largest freshwater lake in the world. It has a surface area of 31,700 square miles. Extending 1,333 feet down at its deepest point, it is also the deepest of the Great Lakes. The lake borders on Minnesota, Wisconsin, Michigan, and Ontario, Canada. Near the city of Sault (pronounced *soo*) Sainte Marie, Michigan, the river is filled with rapids, making ship travel impossible. In order to correct this problem, the government built the Soo Locks, a waterway around the rapids that allows ships to travel between the lakes.

Lake Huron was the first of the Great Lakes to be discovered by white explorers. It was named for the Hurons, a Native American people who once lived on its shores.

The lake, with a surface area of 23,000 square miles, has the longest shoreline of any Great Lake. It is a very scenic shoreline with more islands off the coast than any of the other Great Lakes. Michigan's Mackinac Island and Manitoulin Island in Ontario, Canada, are the two most important islands. Huron's southern end is connected to the western end of Lake Erie by tiny Lake St. Clair.

Lake Huron has been the site of some violent storms, which have at times made shipping dangerous.

Lake Michigan, called *Michi-guma* (big water) by the Native Americans who at one time lived along its shores, covers 22,300 square miles. It is the only Great Lake that lies entirely within the United States.

Lake Michigan, with its many beaches, is a popular recreation area. The lake's main transports are wood products, copper and iron ores, and food supplies.

Lake Michigan and Lake Huron come together naturally. Their meeting point divides the state of Michigan into two parts: the Lower Peninsula, where most of Michigan's big cities are located, and the Upper Peninsula, containing much scenic wilderness.

Jean Nicolet, a French explorer living in Quebec, Canada, was the first European to see this lake. He was sent to the area in 1634 to restore peace between two Native American tribes.

Lake Erie was the last Great Lake to be explored by Europeans. In 1669, Louis Jolliet accidentally came upon it during his search for copper. It was named for the Erie Indians, who lived south of the lake.

The lake covers 9,910 square miles and borders four states—Michigan, Ohio, Pennsylvania, and New

Midway along the Niagara River, water traveling from Lake Erie to Lake Ontario plunges 325 feet over Niagara Falls. Millions of people visit the falls each year to witness their powerful beauty.

York—and Ontario, Canada. It is the shallowest Great Lake and lies farther south than the other Great Lakes. The Niagara River provides a natural waterway between Lake Erie and Lake Ontario. However, because dangerous Niagara Falls prevents ships from traveling between the two lakes, the twenty-six mile Welland Canal was built just west of the falls.

Lake Ontario, with its 7,340 square miles, is the smallest of the Great Lakes. Lying between Ontario, Canada, and New York State, it is also the easternmost of the five lakes. The entire Great Lakes system drains into it.

Ontario was explored in 1615, the same year that Huron was first sighted by the Europeans. It has a number of excellent harbors. Major ports include Rochester and Oswego in New York and Toronto, Kingston, and Hamilton in Canada. Toronto is the largest city on the shores of Lake Ontario.

Land of 10,000 Lakes

One of the states bordering Lake Superior is Minnesota, Land of 10,000 Lakes. Actually, the state has closer to 15,000 lakes; the 10,000 refers to the largest lakes. Minnesota probably has more inland water than any other state—one square mile of water for every twenty square miles of land.

Why does Minnesota have so much water? Thousands of years ago, glaciers covered the area. Over the years, as the glaciers moved northward, they carved the land into lake beds and swamplands.

THE ST. LAWRENCE SEAWAY

The huge task of deepening the St. Lawrence River canal was a joint effort of the United States and Canada. One purpose of the project was to deepen the canal so bigger boats could use it. The other purpose was to build power stations that would produce electricity from the river water.

This canal was not the first in the river's history. The first canal was only 18 inches deep, but it was big enough for the fur traders' canoes. Over the years, bigger and bigger boats made it necessary to enlarge the waterway. Locks, which trap boats in the canal for a few minutes while water is pumped into the trapper section, were added to adjust for different water levels along the river.

In 1932, the St. Lawrence Deep Waterway Treaty was signed, but work did not begin on the St. Lawrence Seaway Project until 1954. Five years later when the new waterway was completed, it provided cheaper and shorter transportation from Europe to major cities in North America. Today the St. Lawrence Seaway is one of the most used transportation routes in the world, and one of the most important sources of electric power.

Melting ice filled the stream and lake beds, giving the state the many waterways that it has today.

Among its more famous bodies of water is Lake Itasca. Located in the north central part of the state, it is the source of the Mississippi River. But other Minnesota lakes are larger than Lake Itasca. On the northern border with Canada is Lake of the Woods, which ranks fortieth in size worldwide. The largest lake that lies entirely within the state is Red Lake, which flows north into Hudson Bay. It covers 451 square miles.

The Great Salt Lake

Far to the west of Minnesota, in the state of Utah, is the Great Salt Lake, the second saltiest body of water in the world. It is located near Salt Lake City, Utah.

Thousands of years ago, during the Ice Age, a lake nearly as large as Lake Michigan covered the area around modern-day Salt Lake City. For 25,000 years the lake was there, its size changing over time. Lake Bonneville, as it was later named, filled with fresh water from the melting ice.

After thousands of years with no outlet (no river or stream flowing out of it) and a small amount of water flowing into it, Lake Bonneville began to dry up, leaving a salty bed. A series of ledges was left around its shoreline. Many of Utah's modern cities have been built on these terraces.

Not all of the water disappeared from Lake Bonneville. The portion that was left became today's Great Salt Lake, the largest and saltiest body of water

A rare view of swimmers in Great Salt Lake. People usually prefer not to swim in the lake because the salt forms a crust on the skin.

in the Western Hemisphere. Like its early ancestor, the lake has no outlet, so it continues to shrink over time. During the last century, its area has shrunk from about 2,400 to about 940 square miles.

Water in the Great Salt Lake is about 25 percent salt—making it nearly six times saltier than the oceans! Only the Dead Sea, between the Asian countries of Israel and Jordan, is saltier. The lake is so salty that it is very difficult for swimmers to drown. The salt keeps their bodies afloat. Few forms of life can live in such water, but the lake is an extremely valuable source of salt.

America's Longest Rivers

1. **Mississippi** 2,348 miles (3,778 km). Source: Lake Itasca, Minnesota; Mouth: Gulf of Mexico
2. **Missouri** 2,315 miles (3,725 km). Source: southwest Montana; Mouth: Mississippi River
3. **Yukon** 1,979 miles (3,184 km). Source: northwestern British Columbia, Canada; Mouth: Bering Sea, Alaska
4. **Rio Grande** 1,800 miles (2,896 km). Source: southwestern Colorado; Mouth: Gulf of Mexico
5. **Arkansas** 1,460 miles (2,349 km). Source: Colorado Rockies; Mouth: Mississippi River
6. **Colorado** 1,450 miles (2,333 km). Source: Colorado Rockies; Mouth: Gulf of California
7. **Red River of the South** 1,300 miles (2,092 km). Source: northern Texas; Mouth: part into the Gulf of Mexico, part into the Mississippi River
8. **Columbia** 1,210 miles (1,947 km). Source: southwestern British Columbia, Canada; Mouth: Pacific Ocean
9. **Snake** 1,038 miles (1,670 km). Source: southern Yellowstone National Park, Wyoming; Mouth: Columbia River

10. **Ohio** 981 miles (1,578 km). Source: Pittsburgh, Pennsylvania; Mouth: Mississippi River
11. **Pecos** 926 miles (1,490 km). Source: north central New Mexico; Mouth: Rio Grande River
12. **Brazos** 870 miles (1,400 km). Source: north central Texas; Mouth: Gulf of Mexico
13. **St. Lawrence** 760 miles (1,223 km). Source: Lake Ontario; Mouth: Gulf of St. Lawrence
14. **Green** 730 miles (1,175 km). Source: west central Wyoming's Wind River Range; Mouth: Colorado River
15. **James** 710 miles (1,142 km). Source: central North Dakota; Mouth: Missouri River
16. **Cimarron** 698 miles (1,123 km). Source: northeastern New Mexico; Mouth: Arkansas River
17. **Cumberland** 687 miles (1,105 km). Source: southern Kentucky; Mouth: Ohio River
18. **Yellowstone** 671 miles (1,080 km). Source: southeast of Yellowstone National Park, Wyoming; Mouth: Missouri River
19. **Tennessee** 652 miles (1,049 km). Source: north of Knoxville, Tennessee; Mouth: Ohio River
20. **Gila River** 650 miles (1,046 km). Source: southwestern New Mexico; Mouth: Colorado River

America's Largest Lakes (in terms of surface area)

1. **Superior** 31,700 sq. mi. (82,100 km^2): Minnesota, Wisconsin, Michigan
2. **Huron** 23,000 sq. mi. (59,600 km^2): Michigan
3. **Michigan** 22,300 sq. mi. (57,800 km^2): Wisconsin, Illinois, Indiana, Michigan
4. **Erie** 9,910 sq. mi. (25,667 km^2): Michigan, Ohio, Pennsylvania, New York
5. **Ontario** 7,340 sq. mi. (19,010 km^2): New York
6. **Great Salt Lake** 1,700 sq. mi. (4,440 km^2) with wide variations: Utah
7. **Lake of the Woods** 1,679 sq mi. (4,349 km^2): Minnesota
8. **Iliamma** 1,000 sq. mi. (2,590 km^2): Alaska
9. **Okeechobee** 700 sq. mi (1,813 km^2): Florida
10. **Pontchartrain** 625 sq. mi. (1,619 km^2): Louisiana

Chronology

1535 Jacques Cartier travels the St. Lawrence River.

1541 Hernando de Soto sights the Mississippi River.

1609 Henry Hudson sails the *Half Moon* up the river that will later bear his name. Henry Spelman, who later explored the James and Potomac Rivers, arrives in the colonies.

1615 Samuel de Champlain reaches the Great Lakes region, sailing into Lake Huron. Lake Ontario is discovered.

1634 French explorer Jean Nicolet sights Lake Michigan.

1673 French explorers Louis Jolliet and Father Jacques Marquette explore the upper Mississippi.

1682 Rene-Robert Cavelier, sieur de La Salle, claims the Mississippi River basin for France.

1786 The Annapolis Convention is called to discuss matters of river travel.

1803- Meriwether Lewis and
1806 William Clark travel along the Ohio, Missouri, Yellowstone, and Columbia rivers to explore the Louisiana Territory, which includes all the land drained by the Mississippi.

1807 Robert Fulton tests his new invention, a steamboat named the *Clermont*, on New York's Hudson River. Traveling along the Yellowstone River, John Colter becomes the first white person to visit future Yellowstone National Park.

1811 Earthquakes change the route of the Mississippi. The *New Orleans* is the first steamboat to travel on the Mississippi River. John Jacob Astor establishes Astoria, a fur-trading post at the mouth of the Columbia River.

1825 The Erie Canal opens across New York State, connecting the Great Lakes with the Atlantic Ocean.

1831 Regular steamboat service begins on the Missouri River.

1869 Explorer John Wesley Powell's expedition is the first to travel the length of the Colorado River by boat.

1897- The Yukon River becomes a
1898 travel route for gold seekers.

1932 The St. Lawrence Deep Waterway Treaty is signed.

1933 President Franklin D. Roosevelt establishes the Tennessee Valley Authority (TVA) to control flooding, produce electric power, and improve navigation on the Tennessee River.

1936 Boulder Dam (later Hoover Dam) is built on the Colorado River on the Arizona-Nevada border, creating Lake Mead.

1959 The St. Lawrence Seaway Project, begun in 1954, is completed, allowing large oceangoing vessels to travel from the Great Lakes along the St. Lawrence and into the Atlantic Ocean.

1964 The Colorado's Glen Canyon Dam is completed, creating Lake Powell.

1993 The most costly flood ($12 billion) in America's history hits a nine-state area drained by the Mississippi River.

For Further Reading

Barrett, Norman S. *Rivers and Lakes.* New York: Franklin Watts, 1989.

Bender, Lionel. *River* (Story of the Earth series). New York: Franklin Watts, 1988.

Emil, Jane. *All About Rivers.* Mahwah, NJ: Troll Associates, 1984.

Morgan, Patricia, J. *A River Adventure.* Mahwah, NJ: Troll Associates, 1988.

Updegraff, Imelda. *Rivers and Lakes.* Mankato, MN: Children's Book Co., 1981.

Index

Allegheny River, 10
Arkansas River, 26–28, 35

Canals, 5, 12, 13, 38
Cavelier, René-Robert. *See* Sieur de La Salle.
Chesapeake Bay, 7, 9, 13
Clemens, Samuel, 21
Colorado River, 5, 31, 32, 33, 34
Colter, John, 28–29
Columbia River, 33, 34
Continental Divide, 5, 29, 33
Cumberland River, 8, 9–10

Dams, 10, 11, 34
Delaware River, 13
de Soto, Henry, 16

Erie Canal, 12

Finn, Huckleberry, 4, 21
Fulton, Robert, 18

Grand Canyon, 31–32, 33
Grand Coulee Dam, 34
Grant, Ulysses S., 9
Great Lakes, 12, 37, 38–41
Great Salt Lake, 37, 43–44
Green River, 32
Gulf of Mexico, 4, 5, 35

Hoover Dam, 34
Hudson, Henry, 12
Hudson River, 8, 12, 18

Intracoastal waterways, 13

James River, 7
Jolliet, Louis, 16

Lake Erie, 12, 37, 39, 40–41
Lake Huron, 37, 39, 40
Lake Itasca, 43
Lake Mead, 34
Lake Michigan, 37, 39–40, 43
Lake of the Woods, 43
Lake Ontario, 8, 37, 40, 41

Lake Superior, 37, 39, 41
Land of 10, 000 lakes, 37, 41, 43
Life on the Mississippi, 21

Marquette, Father Jacques, 16
Mississippi River, 4, 10, 15–17, 18, 19, 22, 23, 26, 33, 43
Missouri River, 15, 17, 18, 22, 23, 25, 29
Monongahela River, 8, 10

Native Americans, 4, 8, 11, 15, 16, 20, 39
Niagara Falls, 40, 41
Niagara River, 40, 41
Nicolet, Jean, 40

Ohio River, 10–11, 17

Penn, William, 13
Pike, Zebulon, 28
Platte River, 25–26
Potomac River, 7, 8, 9
Powell, John Wesley, 33

Red River, 28
Rio Grande, 35
Roosevelt, Franklin D., 11
Roosevelt, Nicholas, 18

Sawyer, Tom, 4, 21
Sieur de La Salle, 16–17
Smith, John, 7
Snake River, 33, 34
Spelman, Henry, 7–8, 9
St. Lawrence Seaway, 42
Susquehanna River, 8, 13

Tennessee River, 8, 9–10
Tennessee Valley Authority (TVA), 11
Twain, Mark, 21. *See also* Samuel Clemens.

Washington, George, 9

Yellowstone Lake, 29
Yellowstone River, 28–29
Yukon River, 35